Easy Pasta Salad Cookbook

50 Delicious Pasta Salad Recipes

By
BookSumo Press

Published by
http://www.booksumo.com

LEGAL NOTES

Table of Contents

Italian Seashells Salad 28

Mexican Style Rotini Salad 29

French Taco Spirals Salad 30

Italian Spring Pasta Salad 31

Salmon Macaroni Salad with Yogurt Dressing 32

Balsamic Romaine Shells Salad 33

Fruity Curry Shells Salad 34

Garbanzo Bows Pasta 35

Broccoli Romano Ravioli Salad 36

Cocktail Shrimp Macaroni Salad 37

Tri-colored Greek Style Pasta Salad 38

Hot Pasta Spirals Salad 39

Rotini Crabmeat Salad 40

Greek Rotini Salad with Lemon Dressing 41

Vegan Rigatoni Basil Salad 42

Minty Feta and Orzo Salad 43

Cheesy Pepperoni Rotini Salad 44

Nutty Chicken Pasta Salad 45

Fresh Lemon Pasta Salad 46

Mashe Tortellini Jarred Salad 47

Italian Chicken Tenders and Farfalle Salad 48

Romano Linguine Pasta Salad 49

Saucy Cheddar Fusilli Salad 50

Neon
Italian Pasta Salad

🥣 Prep Time: 20 mins
🕐 Total Time: 13 hrs 55 mins

Servings per Recipe: 6

Calories	400 kcal
Fat	24.8 g
Carbohydrates	39g
Protein	7.9 g
Cholesterol	3 mg
Sodium	< 1904 mg

Ingredients

1 lb tri-colored spiral pasta
6 tbsp salad seasoning mix
1 (16 oz) bottle Italian-style salad dressing
2 C. cherry tomatoes, diced
1 green bell pepper, chopped

1 red bell pepper, diced
1/2 yellow bell pepper, chopped
1 (2.25 oz) can black olives, chopped

Directions

1. Cook the pasta according to the directions on the package.
2. Get a small mixing bowl: Combine in it the salad seasoning mix with Italian dressing to make the dressing.
3. Get a large mixing bowl: Toss in it dressing with pasta, cherry tomatoes, bell peppers and olives. Place the salad in the fridge for an overnight.
4. Serve it with your favorite toppings.
5. Enjoy.

GENO ASIAGO
Pasta Salad

Prep Time: 20 mins
Total Time: 1 hr 35 mins

Servings per Recipe: 12

Calories	451 kcal
Fat	29.1 g
Carbohydrates	33.2g
Protein	15 g
Cholesterol	37 mg
Sodium	978 mg

Ingredients

1 lb seashell pasta
1/4 lb Genoa salami, chopped
1/4 lb pepperoni sausage, chopped
1/2 lb Asiago cheese, diced
1 (6 oz) can black olives, drained and chopped
1 red bell pepper, diced
1 green bell pepper, chopped
3 tomatoes, chopped
1 (.7 oz) package dry Italian-style salad dressing mix

3/4 C. extra virgin olive oil
1/4 C. balsamic vinegar
2 tbsp dried oregano
1 tbsp dried parsley
1 tbsp grated Parmesan cheese
salt and ground black pepper to taste

Directions

1. Prepare the pasta according to the instructions on the package.
2. Get a small mixing bowl: Combine in it the olive oil, balsamic vinegar, oregano, parsley, Parmesan cheese, salt and pepper. Mix them well.
3. Get a large mixing bowl: Toss in it the remaining ingredients. Drizzle the dressing on top. Chill the salad in the fridge until ready to serve.
4. Enjoy.

Mediterranean
Red Wine Pasta Salad

Prep Time: 15 mins
Total Time: 2 hrs 25 mins

Servings per Recipe: 4
Calories   746 kcal
Fat   56.1 g
Carbohydrates   40.4g
Protein   22.1 g
Cholesterol   70 mg
Sodium   1279 mg

Ingredients

1/2 C. olive oil
1/2 C. red wine vinegar
1 1/2 tsp garlic powder
1 1/2 tsp dried basil
1 1/2 tsp dried oregano
3/4 tsp ground black pepper
3/4 tsp white sugar
2 1/2 C. cooked elbow macaroni
3 C. fresh sliced mushrooms
15 cherry tomatoes, halved
1 C. sliced red bell peppers

3/4 C. crumbled feta cheese
1/2 C. chopped green onions
1 (4 oz) can whole black olives
3/4 C. sliced pepperoni sausage, cut into strips

Directions

1. Get a large mixing bowl: Combine in it the olive oil, vinegar, garlic powder, basil, oregano, black pepper, and sugar. Mix them well.
2. Add the pasta, mushrooms, tomatoes, red peppers, feta cheese, green onions, olives, and pepperoni. Stir them well. Pace the salad in the fridge for 3 h to an overnight.
3. Serve it with your favorite toppings.
4. Enjoy.

PROVOLONE
Pimentos Pasta Salad

Prep Time: 30 mins
Total Time: 40 mins

Servings per Recipe: 16	
Calories	310 kcal
Fat	17.7 g
Carbohydrates	25.9 g
Protein	12.9 g
Cholesterol	31 mg
Sodium	913 mg

Ingredients

1 (16 oz) package Fusilli (spiral) pasta
3 C. cherry tomatoes, halved
1/2 lb provolone cheese, cubed
1/2 lb salami, cubed
1/4 lb sliced pepperoni, cut in half
1 large green bell pepper, cut into 1
inch pieces

1 (10 oz) can black olives, drained
1 (4 oz) jar pimentos, drained
1 (8 oz) bottle Italian salad dressing

Directions

1. Prepare the pasta according to the directions on the package.
2. Get a large mixing bowl: Toss in it the cooked pasta with the remaining ingredients. Serve your salad.
3. Enjoy.

Multi-colored
Pepperoni Pasta Salad with Oregano Dressing

Prep Time: 35 mins
Total Time: 8 hrs 45 mins

Servings per Recipe: 8
Calories	443 kcal
Fat	32 g
Carbohydrates	25.4g
Protein	15.9 g
Cholesterol	39 mg
Sodium	836 mg

Ingredients

1 (8 oz) package uncooked tri-color Rotini pasta
6 oz pepperoni sausage, diced
6 oz provolone cheese, cubed
1 red onion, thinly sliced
1 small cucumber, thinly sliced
3/4 C. chopped green bell pepper
3/4 C. chopped red bell pepper
1 (6 oz) can pitted black olives
1/4 C. minced fresh parsley
1/4 C. grated Parmesan cheese

1/2 C. olive oil
1/4 C. red wine vinegar
2 cloves garlic, minced
1 tsp dried basil
1 tsp dried oregano
1/2 tsp ground mustard seed
1/4 tsp salt
1/8 tsp ground black pepper

Directions

1. Cook the pasta according to the directions on the package.
2. Get a small jar or a small mixing bowl: Combine in it the olive oil, vinegar, garlic, basil, oregano, ground mustard, salt, and pepper. Mix them well to make the dressing.
3. Get a large mixing bowl: Toss in it the dressing with the remaining ingredients. Place the salad in the fridge for an overnight.
4. Adjust the seasoning of the salad then serve it.
5. Enjoy.

FARFALLE
Lemon Salad

Prep Time: 10 mins
Total Time: 2 hrs 25 mins

Servings per Recipe: 8
Calories	334 kcal
Fat	16.6 g
Carbohydrates	41.8g
Protein	8.6 g
Cholesterol	6 mg
Sodium	1167 mg

Ingredients

1 (12 oz) package Farfalle pasta
10 oz baby spinach, rinsed and torn into bite-size piece
2 oz crumbled feta cheese with basil and tomato
1 red onion, chopped
1 (15 oz) can black olives, drained and chopped

1 C. Italian-style salad dressing
4 cloves garlic, minced
1 lemon, juiced
1/2 tsp garlic salt
1/2 tsp ground black pepper

Directions

1. Cook the pasta according to the directions on the package.
2. Get a small mixing bowl: Combine in it the salad dressing, garlic, lemon juice, garlic salt and pepper. Mix them well to make the dressing.
3. Get a large mixing bowl: Combine in it the pasta, spinach, cheese, red onion and olives. Add the dressing and toss them well.
4. Place the salad in the fridge for 3 h to an overnight then serve it.
5. Enjoy.

Greek Style Chicken Pasta Salad

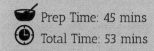 Prep Time: 45 mins

Total Time: 53 mins

Servings per Recipe: 6

Calories	425 kcal
Fat	18.9 g
Carbohydrates	44.7g
Protein	21.8 g
Cholesterol	35 mg
Sodium	358 mg

Ingredients

1 tsp finely chopped, peeled fresh ginger
1/3 C. rice vinegar
1/4 C. orange juice
1/4 C. vegetable oil
1 tsp toasted sesame oil
1 (1 oz) package dry onion soup mix
2 tsp white sugar
1 clove garlic, pressed
1 (8 oz) package bow tie (farfalle) pasta
1/2 cucumber - scored, halved lengthwise, seeded, and sliced

1/2 C. diced red bell pepper
1/2 C. coarsely chopped red onion
2 diced Roma tomatoes
1 carrot, shredded
1 (6 oz) bag fresh spinach
1 (11 oz) can mandarin orange segments, drained
2 C. diced cooked chicken
1/2 C. sliced almonds, toasted

Directions

1. Get a small mixing bowl: Combine in it the ginger root, rice vinegar, orange juice, vegetable oil, sesame oil, soup mix, sugar, and garlic.
2. Mix them well to make the dressing. Place it in the fridge.
3. Cook the pasta according to the directions on the package.
4. Get a large mixing bowl: Combine in it all the ingredients. Drizzle the dressing on top and toss the salad to coat. Adjust the seasoning of the salad and serve it.
5. Enjoy.

PROSCIUTTO
Pasta Salad

Prep Time: 15 mins
Total Time: 30 mins

Servings per Recipe: 10

Calories	372 kcal
Fat	20.7 g
Carbohydrates	36.4g
Protein	13.6 g
Cholesterol	15 mg
Sodium	329 mg

Ingredients

1 (16 oz) package bow tie pasta
1 (6 oz) package spinach leaves
2 C. fresh basil leaves
1/2 C. extra virgin olive oil
3 cloves garlic, minced
4 oz prosciutto, diced

salt and ground black pepper to taste
3/4 C. freshly grated Parmesan cheese
1/2 C. toasted pine nuts

Directions

1. Cook the pasta according to the directions on the package.
2. Place a large pan over medium heat. Heat the oil in it. Add the garlic and cook it for 60 sec. Add the prosciutto and cook them for 4 min.
3. Get a large mixing bowl: Transfer the prosciutto and garlic mix to the mixing bowl with the pasta, spinach, basil, a pinch of salt and pepper. Toss them well.
4. Top your pasta with pine nuts and parmesan. Serve it.
5. Enjoy.

Italian Style
Rotini Salad

🥣 Prep Time: 15 mins

🕐 Total Time: 30 mins

Servings per Recipe: 12

Calories	289 kcal
Fat	13.9 g
Carbohydrates	34.6g
Protein	10 g
Cholesterol	8 mg
Sodium	764 mg

Ingredients

1 (16 oz) package uncooked rotini pasta
1 (16 oz) bottle Italian salad dressing
2 cucumbers, chopped
6 tomatoes, chopped

1 bunch green onions, chopped
4 oz grated Parmesan cheese
1 tbsp Italian seasoning

Directions

1. Cook the pasta according to the directions on the package.
2. Get a large mixing bowl: Combine in it the pasta with the rest of the ingredients. Mix them well. Place your pasta in the fridge until ready to serve.
3. Enjoy.

CHERRY MUENSTER
Pasta Salad

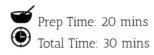

Prep Time: 20 mins
Total Time: 30 mins

Servings per Recipe: 6
Calories	550 kcal
Fat	35.1 g
Carbohydrates	37.3g
Protein	23.7 g
Cholesterol	61 mg
Sodium	1000 mg

Ingredients

8 oz corkscrew-shaped pasta
3/4 C. Italian-style salad dressing
1/4 C. mayonnaise
2 C. chopped, cooked rotisserie chicken
12 slices crispy cooked turkey bacon, crumbled

1 C. cubed Muenster cheese
1 C. chopped celery
1 C. chopped green bell pepper
8 oz cherry tomatoes, halved
1 avocado - peeled, pitted, and chopped

Directions

1. Cook the pasta according to the directions on the package.
2. Get a large mixing bowl: Combine in it the mayo with Italian dressing. Mix them well.
3. Add the remaining ingredients. Toss them to coat. Serve your pasta salad.
4. Enjoy.

Bell Salami
Pasta Salad

Prep Time: 15 mins
Total Time: 25 mins

Servings per Recipe: 12

Calories	371 kcal
Fat	21 g
Carbohydrates	29.2g
Protein	15.2 g
Cholesterol	46 mg
Sodium	1893 mg

Ingredients

1 (12 oz) package tri-color rotini pasta
3/4 lb Italian salami, finely diced
1/2 green bell pepper, sliced
1/2 red bell pepper, sliced
1/2 red onion, chopped
1 C. Italian-style salad dressing

1 (6 oz) can sliced black olives
8 oz small fresh mozzarella balls
3 (.7 oz) packages dry Italian-style salad dressing mix, or to taste
1/2 C. shredded Parmesan cheese

Directions

1. Cook the pasta according to the directions on the package.
2. Get a large mixing bowl: Toss in it the pasta with the rest of the ingredients. Serve your salad with some extra parmesan cheese on top.
3. Enjoy.

CAESAR
Pasta Salad

Prep Time: 15 mins
Total Time: 30 mins

Servings per Recipe: 12
Calories	291 kcal
Fat	14.6 g
Carbohydrates	32.6g
Protein	8.5 g
Cholesterol	6 mg
Sodium	728 mg

Ingredients

1 (16 oz) package rotini pasta
1 C. Italian-style salad dressing
1 C. creamy Caesar salad dressing
1 C. grated Parmesan cheese
1 red bell pepper, diced

1 green bell pepper, chopped
1 red onion, diced

Directions

1. Cook the pasta according to the directions on the package.
2. Get a large mixing bowl: Combine the pasta with the remaining ingredients. Mix them well. Adjust the seasoning of the pasta and serve it.
3. Enjoy.

Creamy Dijon
Pasta Salad

Prep Time: 25 mins

Total Time: 2 hrs 35 mins

Servings per Recipe: 8

Calories	451 kcal
Fat	28.8 g
Carbohydrates	33.8g
Protein	15.4 g
Cholesterol	99 mg
Sodium	664 mg

Ingredients

Dressing:
1 1/4 C. mayonnaise, or more if needed
2 tsp Dijon mustard
2 tsp ketchup
1/4 tsp Worcestershire sauce
1 tsp salt, or to taste
1 pinch cayenne pepper, or to taste
1 lemon, juiced
1/3 C. chopped fresh dill
Salad:
1 (12 oz) package small pasta shells

1 lb cooked, peeled, and deveined small shrimp
- cut in half
1/2 C. finely diced red bell pepper
3/4 C. diced celery
salt and ground black pepper to taste
1 pinch paprika, for garnish
3 sprigs fresh dill, or as desired

Directions

1. Get a small mixing bowl: Combine in it 1 1/4 C. mayonnaise, Dijon mustard, ketchup, Worcestershire sauce, salt, and cayenne pepper. Mix them well.
2. Fold in the lemon juice and 1/3 C. chopped dill to make the dressing. Place it in the fridge.
3. Cook the pasta according to the directions on the package.
4. Get a large mixing bowl: Combine in it the pasta with shrimp, red bell pepper, celery, and dressing . Mix them well.
5. Wrap a piece of plastic over the bowl. Place it in the fridge for 2 h 30 min. Stir in the lemon juice with cayenne pepper. Adjust the seasoning of the salad then serve it.
6. Enjoy.

ROASTED
Pasta Hearts Salad

Prep Time: 30 mins
Total Time: 2 hrs 40 mins

Servings per Recipe: 10
Calories	358 kcal
Fat	17.1 g
Carbohydrates	38.2g
Protein	13.5 g
Cholesterol	24 mg
Sodium	1375 mg

Ingredients

1 (16 oz) package tri-color rotini pasta
1 small red onion, diced
1 C. diced roasted red peppers
1 C. cubed mozzarella cheese
1 (6 oz) jar marinated artichoke hearts, drained and chopped
1/4 lb salami, diced
3/4 C. sliced stuffed green olives
1 (4 oz) can sliced black olives
1/2 C. sliced pepperoncini peppers (optional)

1 tsp Italian seasoning
1/4 tsp garlic powder, or to taste
1 pinch seasoned salt, or to taste
ground black pepper to taste
1/3 C. Italian-style salad dressing
1/4 C. mayonnaise
1/2 C. shredded Parmesan cheese

Directions

1. Cook the pasta according to the directions on the package.
2. Get a small mixing bowl: Combine in it the Italian-style dressing and mayonnaise. Mix them well.
3. Get a large mixing bowl: Combine in it the Rotini, red onion, roasted red peppers, mozzarella cheese, artichoke hearts, salami, green olives, black olives, Pepperoncini peppers, Italian seasoning, garlic powder, seasoned salt, and black pepper.
4. Drizzle the dressing on top. Serve your salad.
5. Enjoy.

Blue Chicken
Rotini Salad

Prep Time: 20 mins
Total Time: 1 hr 30 mins

Servings per Recipe: 12
Calories	379 kcal
Fat	21.1 g
Carbohydrates	34.6g
Protein	13.6 g
Cholesterol	40 mg
Sodium	1051 mg

Ingredients

1 (16 oz) package uncooked rotini pasta
1/2 C. mayonnaise
1 C. chunky blue cheese dressing
1/2 C. buffalo wing sauce
1 tsp salt
1/2 tsp black pepper

1 lb frozen cooked chicken strips, defrosted and diced
1/2 C. red bell pepper, diced
1/2 C. green bell pepper, diced
1 C. red onion, diced

Directions

1. Cook the pasta according to the directions on the package.
2. Get a large mixing bowl: Combine in it the mayonnaise, blue cheese dressing, buffalo wing sauce, salt and pepper. Whisk them well.
3. Stir in the chicken, bell peppers, red onion, and cooked pasta. Mix them well. Place the salad in the fridge for 1 h 15 min. Serve it.
4. Enjoy.

GREEK
Rotini Salad

Prep Time: 15 mins
Total Time: 2 hrs 30 mins

Servings per Recipe: 8
Calories	297 kcal
Fat	10.6 g
Carbohydrates	43.9g
Protein	7.2 g
Cholesterol	0 mg
Sodium	608 mg

Ingredients

14 oz uncooked rotini pasta
2 cucumbers, chopped
1/2 onion, finely chopped
10 cherry tomatoes, quartered

3/4 C. pitted black olives, sliced
1 C. Italian-style salad dressing

Directions

1. Cook the pasta according to the directions on the package.
2. Get a large mixing bowl: Toss in it the pasta with the cucumbers, onion, tomatoes, and olives . Add the Italian dressing and stir them well.
3. Wrap a piece of plastic wrap on the bowl and place it in the fridge for 2 h 30 min. Serve it.
4. Enjoy.

Corn and Chicken
Flakes Salad

🍲 Prep Time: 30 mins
🕐 Total Time: 40 mins

Servings per Recipe: 6
Calories	458 kcal
Fat	33.3 g
Carbohydrates	26.6g
Protein	15.8 g
Cholesterol	48 mg
Sodium	1078 mg

Ingredients

1/2 lb rotini/corkscrew pasta
1/2 C. sliced fresh mushrooms
1/2 C. sliced green olives
1 stalk celery, chopped
1/4 C. minced onion
1 C. shredded Cheddar cheese
1 (10 oz) package frozen corn kernels

1 green bell pepper, chopped
3/4 C. Italian-style salad dressing
1/2 C. mayonnaise
1 C. canned chicken meat - drained and flaked
salt and pepper to taste

Directions

1. Cook the pasta according to the directions on the package.
2. Get a small mixing bowl: Combine in it the dressing and mayonnaise. Mix them well.
3. Get a large mixing bowl: Toss in it the mushrooms, olives, celery, onion, cheese, corn and green bell pepper with pasta.
4. Add the dressing and mix the well. Fold in the flakes chicken. Place the salad in the fridge until ready to serve.
5. Enjoy.

GRILL ROMAINE
Rotini Salad

Prep Time: 15 mins
Total Time: 45 mins

Servings per Recipe: 4
Calories	504 kcal
Fat	13.2 g
Carbohydrates	48g
Protein	46.5 g
Cholesterol	103 mg
Sodium	650 mg

Ingredients

4 skinless, boneless chicken breast
halves
steak seasoning to taste
8 oz rotini pasta
8 oz mozzarella cheese, cubed
1 red onion, chopped

1 head romaine lettuce, chopped
6 cherry tomatoes, chopped

Directions

1. Before you do anything preheat the grill. Grease its grates.
2. Sprinkle some salt, pepper and steak seasoning on the chicken breasts. Cook them in the grill for 7 to 9 min on each side.
3. Cook the pasta according to the directions on the package.
4. Get a large mixing bowl: Combine in it the cheese, onion, lettuce, and tomatoes. Stir them well. Add the pasta and mix them again.
5. Cut the grill chicken into stripes. Lay the chicken on the pasta salad and serve it.
6. Enjoy.

Bows Pasta Salad
With Sesame Dressing

Prep Time: 20 mins
Total Time: 30 mins

Servings per Recipe: 10

Calories	349 kcal
Fat	15.2 g
Carbohydrates	38.3g
Protein	15.9 g
Cholesterol	24 mg
Sodium	308 mg

Ingredients

1/4 C. sesame seeds
1 (16 oz) package bow tie pasta
1/2 C. vegetable oil
1/3 C. light soy sauce
1/3 C. rice vinegar
1 tsp sesame oil
3 tbsp white sugar

1/2 tsp ground ginger
1/4 tsp ground black pepper
3 C. shredded, cooked chicken breast meat
1/3 C. chopped fresh cilantro
1/3 C. chopped green onion

Directions

1. Place a large pan over medium heat. Cook in it the sesame seeds until they are slightly toasted. Place them aside.
2. Cook the pasta according to the directions on the package.
3. Get a small bowl or a jar: Place in it the vegetable oil, soy sauce, vinegar, sesame oil, sugar, sesame seeds, ginger, and pepper. Mix them well to make the dressing.
4. Get a large mixing bowl: Combine in it the pasta with the sesame dressing, chicken, cilantro, and green onions, a pinch of salt and pepper.
5. Toss them well. Adjust the seasoning of the salad then serve it
6. Enjoy.

BELL BASIL
Colored Pasta Salad

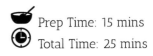

Prep Time: 15 mins

Total Time: 25 mins

Servings per Recipe: 8
Calories	483 kcal
Fat	25.2 g
Carbohydrates	48g
Protein	16.2 g
Cholesterol	19 mg
Sodium	631 mg

Ingredients

1 (16 oz) package tri-color pasta
2/3 C. olive oil
3 tbsp white wine vinegar
1/4 C. fresh basil leaves
2 tbsp grated Parmesan cheese
1 1/4 tsp salt
1/4 tsp ground black pepper
1 red bell pepper, julienned

1 yellow bell pepper, julienned
1 orange bell pepper, julienned
1 medium fresh tomato, chopped
1 (2.25 oz) can black olives, drained
8 oz mozzarella cheese, cubed

Directions

1. Cook the pasta according to the directions on the package.
2. Get a food processor: Combine in it the olive oil, white wine vinegar, basil, Parmesan cheese, salt, and pepper. Process them until they become smooth to make the dressing.
3. Get a large mixing bowl: Combine in it the pasta, dressing, red bell pepper, yellow bell pepper, orange bell pepper, tomato, and olives. Stir them well.
4. Garnish the salad with mozzarella cheese then serve it.
5. Enjoy.

Marinated
Rotini Salami Salad

🥣 Prep Time: 30 mins
🕐 Total Time: 1 hr 40 mins

Servings per Recipe: 8
Calories	720 kcal
Fat	43.2 g
Carbohydrates	53.2g
Protein	29.9 g
Cholesterol	87 mg
Sodium	2597 mg

Ingredients

1 (16 oz) package rotini pasta
2 carrots, peeled and cut into 1/2-inch cubes
1 C. chopped pepperoncini (optional)
1/2 lb Genoa salami, cut into 1/2-inch cubes
1/2 lb Cheddar cheese, cut into 1/2-inch cubes
1/3 lb provolone cheese, cut into 1/2-inch cubes
1/2 sweet onion, cut into 1/2-inch pieces
1/2 C. 1/2-inch pieces pitted green olives
1/2 C. 1/2-inch pieces Kalamata olives

1/2 C. 1/2-inch pieces pepperoni
1/2 C. 1/2-inch pieces celery
1/2 C. chopped green bell pepper
1/2 C. chopped red bell pepper
1/2 (6 oz) jar marinated artichoke hearts, drained and cut into 1/2-inch pieces
1 (8 oz) bottle Italian-style salad dressing, or more to taste

Directions

1. Cook the pasta according to the directions on the package.
2. Get a large mixing bowl: Combine in it the Pepperoncini, Genoa salami, Cheddar cheese, provolone cheese, sweet onion, green olives, Kalamata olives, pepperoni, celery, green bell pepper, red bell pepper, and artichoke hearts.
3. Stir them well. Add the pasta with Italian dressing. Mix them well.
4. Place a plastic wrap over the bowl and place it in the fridge. Chill the salad in the fridge for 1 h 30 min. Adjust the seasoning of the salad and serve it.
5. Enjoy.

ITALIAN
Seashells Salad

Prep Time: 10 mins
Total Time: 2 hrs 25 mins

Servings per Recipe: 6
Calories   218 kcal
Fat   11.4 g
Carbohydrates   20.4g
Protein   9.6 g
Cholesterol   18 mg
Sodium   654 mg

Ingredients

1 C. seashell pasta
1 C. chopped, cooked chicken meat
3 green onions, chopped into 1 inch pieces
1 red bell pepper, chopped
1 C. sliced black olives

1 cucumber, peeled and chopped
2/3 C. Italian-style salad dressing
1/4 C. sunflower seeds (optional)

Directions

1. Cook the pasta according to the directions on the package.
2. Get a large mixing bowl: Stir in it the pasta, chicken, green onions, bell pepper, olives and cucumber.
3. Drizzle the Italian dressing on top. Toss the salad to coat. Place the salad in the fridge for 3 h. Garnish it with some sunflower seeds then serve it.
4. Enjoy.

Mexican Style
Rotini Salad

🥣 Prep Time: 15 mins
🕐 Total Time: 25 mins

Servings per Recipe: 12

Calories	246 kcal
Fat	5.5 g
Carbohydrates	41g
Protein	8.8 g
Cholesterol	5 mg
Sodium	651 mg

Ingredients

1 (16 oz) package tri-color rotini pasta
1 (15 oz) can black beans, drained and rinsed
1 (11 oz) can Mexican-style corn, drained
1 (4 oz) can chopped green chilies
1/2 C. chopped red bell pepper
1/2 C. Italian-style salad dressing, or more to taste

1/2 C. shredded Mexican cheese blend
3 green onions, thinly sliced
1/3 C. minced fresh cilantro
1 slice onion, minced
2 tbsp taco seasoning mix
1/2 lime, juiced

Directions

1. Cook the pasta according to the directions on the package.
2. Get a large mixing bowl: Combine in it the black beans, corn, green chilies, red bell pepper, Italian dressing, Mexican cheese, green onions, cilantro, onion, taco seasoning, and lime juice together.
3. Stir them well. Fold in the pasta. Adjust the seasoning of the salad then serve it.
4. Enjoy.

FRENCH TACO
Spirals Salad

Prep Time: 10 mins
Total Time: 40 mins

Servings per Recipe: 6
Calories	618 kcal
Fat	38.4 g
Carbohydrates	46.4g
Protein	22.8 g
Cholesterol	68 mg
Sodium	980 mg

Ingredients

2 C. spiral pasta
1 lb ground beef
1 (1.25 oz) package taco seasoning
3 C. shredded lettuce
2 C. halved cherry tomatoes
1 C. shredded Cheddar cheese

1/2 C. chopped onion
1/2 C. French salad dressing
1 (7 oz) bag corn chips
2 tbsp sour cream

Directions

1. Cook the pasta according to the directions on the package.
2. Place a large pan over medium heat. Brown in it the beef for 12 min. Discard the excess grease. Add the taco seasoning and mix them well.7
3. Get a large mixing bowl: Transfer to it the beef mix with pasta; toss lettuce, tomatoes, Cheddar cheese, onion, French dressing, and corn chips.
4. Stir them well. Serve your salad with some sour cream.
5. Enjoy.

Italian
Spring Pasta Salad

🥣 Prep Time: 20 mins
🕐 Total Time: 20 mins

Servings per Recipe: 8
Calories   233 kcal
Fat   12.2 g
Carbohydrates   26.2g
Protein   6.6 g
Cholesterol   9 mg
Sodium   598 mg

Ingredients

8 oz rotelle or spiral pasta, cooked and drained
2 1/2 C. assorted cut-up vegetables (broccoli, carrots, tomatoes, bell peppers, cauliflower, onions and mushrooms)

1/2 C. cubed Cheddar or mozzarella cheese
1/3 C. sliced pitted ripe olives (optional)
1 C. Wish-Bone(R) Italian Dressing

Directions

1. Get a large mixing bowl: Combine in it the pasta with veggies, cheddar cheese and olives. Toss them well.
2. Drizzle the dressing on top. Adjust the seasoning of the salad and serve it.
3. Enjoy.

FRUITY SALMON
Macaroni Salad with Yogurt Dressing

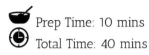 Prep Time: 10 mins
Total Time: 40 mins

Servings per Recipe: 8
Calories	222 kcal
Fat	12.3 g
Carbohydrates	17.6g
Protein	11 g
Cholesterol	18 mg
Sodium	208 mg

Ingredients

1 C. dry pasta, such as macaroni or small shells
8 oz cooked, skinned salmon
1/2 C. minced red or yellow onion
1 C. diced celery
1 medium red apple, diced
1/2 C. chopped walnuts or dry-roasted, unsalted peanuts
Dressing:
1 (6 oz) container fat-free yogurt

2 tbsp olive oil
1 tbsp curry powder
2 tsp fresh lemon juice
2 cloves garlic, crushed
1 tsp Dijon mustard
1/2 tsp salt (or to taste)
Freshly ground black pepper, to taste

Directions

1. Cook the pasta according to the directions on the package.
2. Get a small mixing bowl: Combine in it the dressing ingredients. Mix them well.
3. Get a large mixing bowl: Combine in it the salad ingredients. Add the dressing and stir them well.
4. Adjust the seasoning of the salad. Place it in the fridge until ready to serve.
5. Enjoy.

Balsamic Romaine Shells Salad

Prep Time: 20 mins
Total Time: 30 mins

Servings per Recipe: 9
Calories	312 kcal
Fat	14.7 g
Carbohydrates	30.7g
Protein	14.3 g
Cholesterol	32 mg
Sodium	819 mg

Ingredients

18 jumbo pasta shells
1/2 lb thinly sliced salami
4 C. chopped romaine lettuce
1 C. chopped roma tomatoes
3/4 C. seeded and chopped cucumber

3/4 C. chopped red onion
1/2 C. balsamic vinaigrette salad dressing
1 C. shredded Parmesan cheese

Directions

1. Cook the pasta according to the directions on the package.
2. Get a large mixing bowl: Toss in it the pasta with salami, romaine lettuce, roma tomatoes, cucumber, and red onion. Drizzle the balsamic vinegar on top.
3. Mix them well. Spoon the mix into the pasta shells to stuff them with it. Place the pasta shells on a serving shallow bowl. Sprinkle the cheese on top then serve it.
4. Enjoy.

FRUITY CURRY
Shells Salad

🍲 Prep Time: 25 mins
🕐 Total Time: 1 hr 40 mins

Servings per Recipe: 8
Calories	374 kcal
Fat	32.2 g
Carbohydrates	17.6g
Protein	5.1 g
Cholesterol	10 mg
Sodium	515 mg

Ingredients

8 slices turkey bacon
1/2 C. uncooked shell pasta
2 tbsp white vinegar
1/4 C. white sugar
1 1/2 tbsp dried basil
1 tbsp dried thyme
4 cloves garlic, peeled
1 tsp salt
1 tsp curry powder
1/2 tsp ground black pepper

1 C. canola oil
4 peaches, peeled and cut into chunks
1/2 C. chopped fresh parsley
1/2 C. sliced celery
1/2 C. chopped red bell pepper
6 green onions, chopped

Directions

1. Place a large pan over medium heat. Cook in it the bacon for 12 min until it becomes crisp.
2. Remove it from the grease and place it aside to drain and lose heat. Press the bacon until it becomes crumbled and place it aside.
3. Cook the pasta according to the directions on the package.
4. Get a food processor: Combine in it the vinegar, sugar, basil, thyme, garlic, salt, curry powder, and black pepper. Process them until they become smooth.
5. Add to it the oil in a steady stream while blending all the time until the dressing becomes creamy.
6. Get a large mixing bowl: Toss in it the pasta with bacon, dressing, peaches, parsley, celery, red bell pepper, and green onions.
7. Adjust the seasoning of the salad. Place the salad in the fridge for 1 h 10 min then serve it.
8. Enjoy.

Garbanzo
Bows Pasta

🥣 Prep Time: 18 mins
🕐 Total Time: 30 mins

Servings per Recipe: 10

Calories	207 kcal
Fat	14.5 g
Carbohydrates	15.5g
Protein	4.5 g
Cholesterol	11 mg
Sodium	414 mg

Ingredients

2 1/2 C. bow tie (farfalle) pasta
1 C. Greek salad dressing
2 1/2 tbsp mayonnaise
4 radishes, finely chopped
1/2 cucumber, peeled and chopped

1 (15 oz) can garbanzo beans, drained
3/4 C. crumbled feta cheese

Directions

1. Cook the pasta according to the directions on the package.
2. Get a large mixing bowl: Combine in it the Greek dressing and mayonnaise. Mix them well. Stir in the pasta.
3. Add the radishes, cucumber, garbanzo beans, and crumbled feta cheese and stir them gently. Adjust the seasoning of the salad then serve it.
4. Enjoy.

BROCCOLI ROMANO
Ravioli Salad

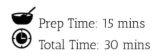

Prep Time: 15 mins
Total Time: 30 mins

Servings per Recipe: 4	
Calories	653 kcal
Fat	31.7 g
Carbohydrates	66.9g
Protein	28 g
Cholesterol	63 mg
Sodium	902 mg

Ingredients

2 (9 oz) packages BUITONI(R) Refrigerated Light Four Cheese Ravioli, prepared according to package directions, chilled
1/4 C. extra virgin olive oil
4 large cloves garlic, finely chopped
1/4 C. red wine vinegar
2 medium tomatoes, chopped
2 C. broccoli florets
1 large green bell pepper, chopped

1/2 C. pitted and halved ripe olives
1/2 C. BUITONI(R) Refrigerated Freshly Shredded Parmesan Cheese
1/4 C. BUITONI(R) Refrigerated Freshly Shredded Romano Cheese

Directions

1. Place a large saucepan over medium heat: Heat the oil in it. Add the garlic and cook it for 60 min.
2. Get a large mixing bowl: Transfer the garlic mix to it and allow it to lose heat for few minutes. Add the vinegar and mix them well.
3. Combine in the pasta, tomatoes, broccoli, bell pepper, olives, Parmesan cheese and Romano cheese. Mix them well.
4. Adjust the seasoning of the pasta. Serve it right away.
5. Enjoy.

Cocktail Shrimp
Macaroni Salad

🥣 Prep Time: 20 mins
🕐 Total Time: 1 hr 30 mins

Servings per Recipe: 6
Calories	528 kcal
Fat	41 g
Carbohydrates	31.9 g
Protein	9.5 g
Cholesterol	56 mg
Sodium	920 mg

Ingredients

1/2 (12 oz) package elbow macaroni
2 stalks celery, coarsely chopped
1 onion, finely chopped
1 cucumber - peeled, seeded, and diced
1 tomato, diced

1 C. cooked small shrimp
1 C. Italian salad dressing
1 C. mayonnaise, or to taste

Directions

1. Cook the pasta according to the directions on the package.
2. Get a large mixing bowl: Combine in it the pasta with celery, onion, cucumber, tomato, shrimp, and Italian salad dressing.
3. Place the salad in the fridge for 1 h 30 min. Stir in the mayo. Adjust the seasoning of the salad then serve it right away.
4. Enjoy.

TRI-COLORED
Greek Style Pasta Salad

 Prep Time: 30 mins

Total Time: 5 hrs 10 mins

Servings per Recipe: 8
Calories	248 kcal
Fat	12.7 g
Carbohydrates	24.9 g
Protein	9 g
Cholesterol	9 mg
Sodium	482 mg

Ingredients

1/2 red onion, cut into bite-size pieces
4 C. ice water, or as needed
1 (8 oz) package tri-color rotini pasta
1 (5 oz) can light tuna in water, drained and flaked
2 stalks celery, cut into bite-size pieces
1/2 C. roasted red peppers, drained and chopped
1/4 C. smoked sun-dried tomatoes
1/4 C. crumbled feta cheese

1 sprig parsley, stemmed and leaves minced
4 leaves fresh basil, rolled and very thinly sliced
2 tsp capers
1 C. Greek vinaigrette salad dressing

Directions

1. Get a large bowl and fill it with ice water. Place the red onion in it and place it in the fridge for 35 min. Remove the onion from the water.
2. Cook the pasta according to the directions on the package.
3. Get a large mixing bowl: Combine in it the onion, pasta, tuna, celery, roasted red peppers, sun-dried tomatoes, feta cheese, parsley, basil, capers, and Greek dressing.
4. Stir them well. Place the salad in the fridge for 5 h to an overnight. Serve your salad with your favorite toppings.
5. Enjoy.

Hot Pasta
Spirals Salad

Prep Time: 20 mins
Total Time: 2 hrs 30 mins

Servings per Recipe: 8	
Calories	190 kcal
Fat	7.4 g
Carbohydrates	27.1g
Protein	4.7 g
Cholesterol	0 mg
Sodium	336 mg

Ingredients

1 (8 oz) package pasta spirals
1/4 C. diced sweet onion
1 green bell pepper, seeded and minced
1/2 fresh hot chile pepper, seeded and minced
2 tomatoes, seeded and chopped
1 cucumber, seeded and chopped
1/4 C. olive oil
1/4 C. tomato sauce

1/4 C. lime juice
3 tbsp red wine vinegar
1 tsp garlic powder
1 tsp salt
ground black pepper to taste

Directions

1. Cook the pasta according to the directions on the package.
2. Get a small mixing bowl: Combine in it the olive oil, tomato sauce, lime juice, red wine vinegar, garlic powder, salt, and black pepper. Mix them well to make the dressing.
3. Get a large mixing bowl: Combine in tit the pasta, sweet onion, green bell pepper, chile pepper, tomatoes, and cucumber.
4. Drizzle the dressing on top and toss the salad well. Adjust the seasoning of the salad and place it in the fridge for 2 h 30 min then serve it.
5. Enjoy.

ROTINI
Crabmeat Salad

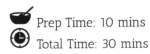 Prep Time: 10 mins

Total Time: 30 mins

Servings per Recipe: 12

Calories	178 kcal
Fat	2 g
Carbohydrates	33.6g
Protein	6.2 g
Cholesterol	4 mg
Sodium	373 mg

Ingredients

1 (12 oz) package rotini pasta
1 (10 oz) package frozen peas, thawed
1 (8 oz) can water chestnuts, chopped
1 (8 oz) package imitation crabmeat,
coarsely chopped - or more to taste
1 C. reduced-fat mayonnaise

2 tbsp chopped fresh chives
1 tbsp chopped fresh dill

Directions

1. Cook the pasta according to the directions on the package.
2. Get a large mixing bowl: Combine in it all the ingredients. Toss them well. Adjust the seasoning of the salad then serve it.
3. Enjoy.

39

Greek Rotini Salad
with Lemon Dressing

Prep Time: 20 mins
Total Time: 9 hrs 33 mins

Servings per Recipe: 8
Calories	453 kcal
Fat	24.9 g
Carbohydrates	50g
Protein	8.9 g
Cholesterol	8 mg
Sodium	1539 mg

Ingredients

1 (16 oz) package tri-color rotini pasta
3 1/2 tbsp lemon juice
2 1/2 tbsp canola oil
3/4 C. mayonnaise
2 1/2 tbsp seasoned salt
1 1/4 tsp flavor enhancer
2 cucumbers, seeded and diced
2 tomatoes, seeded and diced

1 (5 oz) jar sliced pimento-stuffed green olives
1 (3 oz) can chopped black olives
1/4 C. chopped green bell pepper
1/4 C. chopped green onions

Directions

1. Cook the pasta according to the directions on the package.
2. Get a small mixing bowl: Combine in it the lemon juice and canola oil. Mix them well. Add the mayonnaise, seasoned salt, and flavor enhancer then mix them again.
3. Get a large mixing bowl: Toss in it the pasta with dressing. Place it the fridge for an overnight.
4. Add the cucumbers, tomatoes, green olives, black olives, green bell pepper, and green onions to the pasta mix. Toss them well.
5. Adjust the seasoning of the salad then serve it.
6. Enjoy.

VEGAN
Rigatoni Basil Salad

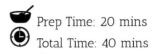 Prep Time: 20 mins

Total Time: 40 mins

Servings per Recipe: 6

Calories	387 kcal
Fat	16.7 g
Carbohydrates	47.8g
Protein	11.9 g
Cholesterol	0 mg
Sodium	89 mg

Ingredients

1 1/2 (8 oz) packages rigatoni pasta
2 tbsp olive oil
2 cloves garlic, minced
1/2 (16 oz) package tofu, drained and cubed
1/2 tsp dried thyme
1 1/2 tsp soy sauce
1 small onion, thinly sliced

1 large tomato, cubed
1 carrot, shredded
6 leaves fresh basil, thinly sliced
6 sprigs fresh cilantro, minced
1/4 C. olive oil

Directions

1. Cook the pasta according to the directions on the package.
2. Place a large pan over medium heat. Heat 2 tbsp of olive oil in it. Add the garlic and cook it for 1 min 30 sec.
3. Stir in the thyme with tofu. Cook them for 9 min. Stir in the soy sauce and turn off the heat.
4. Get a large mixing bowl: Toss in it the rigatoni, tofu mix, onion, tomato, carrot, basil, and cilantro. Drizzle the olive oil over the pasta salad then serve it.
5. Enjoy.

Minty Feta and Orzo Salad

🥣 Prep Time: 30 mins
🕐 Total Time: 2 hrs 50 mins

Servings per Recipe: 8
Calories	374 kcal
Fat	19 g
Carbohydrates	38.2g
Protein	13.3 g
Cholesterol	25 mg
Sodium	456 mg

Ingredients

1 1/4 C. orzo pasta
6 tbsp olive oil, divided
3/4 C. dried brown lentils, rinsed and drained
1/3 C. red wine vinegar
3 cloves garlic, minced
1/2 C. kalamata olives, pitted and chopped
1 1/2 C. crumbled feta cheese

1 small red onion, diced
1/2 C. finely chopped fresh mint leaves
1/2 C. chopped fresh dill
salt and pepper to taste

Directions

1. Cook the pasta according to the directions on the package.
2. Bring a salted large saucepan of water to a boil. Cook in it the lentils until it starts boiling.
3. Lower the heat and put on the lid. Cook the lentils for 22 min. Remove them from the water.
4. Get a small mixing bowl: Combine in it the olive oil, vinegar, and garlic. Whisk them well to make the dressing.
5. Get a large mixing bowl: Toss in it the lentils, dressing, olives, feta cheese, red onion, mint, and dill, with salt and pepper.
6. Wrap a plastic wrap on the salad bowl and place it in the fridge for 2 h 30 min. Adjust the seasoning of the salad then serve it.
7. Enjoy.

CHEESY PEPPERONI
Rotini Salad

Prep Time: 15 mins
Total Time: 1 hr 25 mins

Servings per Recipe: 8

Calories	415 kcal
Fat	29.1 g
Carbohydrates	25.6g
Protein	13.9 g
Cholesterol	33 mg
Sodium	1518 mg

Ingredients

1 (16 oz) package tri-color rotini pasta
1/4 lb sliced pepperoni sausage
1 C. fresh broccoli florets
1 (6 oz) can black olives, drained and sliced
1 (8 oz) package mozzarella cheese, shredded

1 (16 oz) bottle Italian-style salad dressing

Directions

1. Cook the pasta according to the directions on the package.
2. Get a large mixing bowl: Toss in it the pasta, pepperoni, broccoli, olives, cheese and dressing.
3. Adjust the seasoning of the salad and place it in the fridge for 1 h 10 min. Serve it.
4. Enjoy.

Nutty Chicken Pasta Salad

🥣 Prep Time: 20 mins
🕐 Total Time: 1 hr 40 mins

Servings per Recipe: 4	
Calories	475 kcal
Fat	17.4 g
Carbohydrates	57.6 g
Protein	23.7 g
Cholesterol	36 mg
Sodium	644 mg

Ingredients

6 slices turkey bacon
10 asparagus spears, ends trimmed
1/2 (16 oz) package rotini, elbow, or penne pasta
3 tbsp low fat mayonnaise
3 tbsp balsamic vinaigrette salad dressing
2 tsp lemon juice
1 tsp Worcestershire sauce

1 (6 oz) jar marinated artichoke hearts, drained and coarsely chopped
1 cooked chicken breast, cubed
1/4 C. dried cranberries
1/4 C. toasted sliced almonds
salt and pepper to taste

Directions

1. Place a large pan over medium heat. Cook in it the bacon until it becomes crisp. Remove it from the excess grease. Crumble it and place it aside.
2. Cook the pasta according to the directions on the package.
3. Get a small mixing bowl: Combine in it the mayo, balsamic vinaigrette, lemon juice, and Worcestershire sauce. Mix them well.
4. Get a large mixing bowl: Toss in it the pasta with dressing. Add the artichoke, chicken, cranberries, almonds, crumbled bacon, and asparagus, a pinch of salt and pepper.
5. Stir them well. Chill the salad in the fridge for 1 h 10 min then serve it.
6. Enjoy.

46

FRESH LEMON
Pasta Salad

🥣 Prep Time: 15 mins
🕐 Total Time: 1 hr 38 mins

Servings per Recipe: 8
Calories   304 kcal
Fat   8.5 g
Carbohydrates   46.8g
Protein   9.9 g
Cholesterol   4 mg
Sodium   466 mg

Ingredients

1 (16 oz) package tri-color rotini pasta
2 tomatoes, seeded and diced
2 cucumbers - peeled, seeded, and diced
1 (4 oz) can sliced black olives
1/2 C. Italian dressing, or more to taste
1/2 C. shredded Parmesan cheese

1 pinch salt and ground black pepper to taste
1 avocado, diced
1 squeeze lemon juice

Directions

1. Cook the pasta according to the directions on the package.
2. Get a large mixing bowl: Combine in it the pasta, tomatoes, cucumbers, olives, Italian dressing, Parmesan cheese, salt, and pepper. Stir them well.
3. Place the pasta in the fridge for 1 h 15 min.
4. Get a small mixing bowl: Stir in it the lemon juice with avocado. Toss the avocado with pasta salad then serve it.
5. Enjoy.

Mashe Tortellini
Jarred Salad

Prep Time: 20 mins
Total Time: 40 mins

Servings per Recipe: 2
Calories	719 kcal
Fat	39.1 g
Carbohydrates	66.6g
Protein	29.2 g
Cholesterol	76 mg
Sodium	1027 mg

Ingredients

1 (9 oz) package spinach and cheese
tortellini
1 (4 oz) jar pesto
1/4 C. halved, seeded, and sliced English
cucumber
1/4 C. halved cherry tomatoes
1/4 C. matchstick-sized pieces red onion

1/2 C. chopped mache
1 canning jar
salt and ground black pepper to taste

Directions

1. Cook the pasta according to the directions on the package.
2. Spread the pesto in the jar then top it with the cucumbers, tomatoes, onions, tortellini, and mache. Season them with some salt and pepper.
3. Serve your salad right away or refrigerate it until you are ready to serve it.
4. Enjoy.

ITALIAN STYLE
Chicken Tenders and Farfalle Salad

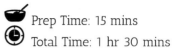 Prep Time: 15 mins
Total Time: 1 hr 30 mins

Servings per Recipe: 6
Calories	542 kcal
Fat	18.4 g
Carbohydrates	67.7g
Protein	29.4 g
Cholesterol	195 mg
Sodium	733 mg

Ingredients

6 eggs
1 (16 oz) package farfalle (bow tie) pasta
6 chicken tenders
1 cucumber, sliced
1 bunch radishes, trimmed and sliced
2 carrots, peeled and sliced

3 green onions, thinly sliced
1/2 red onion, chopped
1/2 (16 oz) bottle Italian-style salad dressing
4 romaine lettuce hearts, thinly sliced

Directions

1. Place the eggs in a large saucepan and cover them with water. Cook the eggs over medium heat until they start boiling.
2. Turn off the heat and let the eggs sit for 16 min. Rinse the eggs with some cold water to make them lose heat.
3. Peel the eggs and slice them then place them aside.
4. Place the chicken tenders in a large saucepan. Cover them with 1/4 C. of water. Cook them over medium heat until the chicken is done.
5. Drain the chicken tenders and cut them into small pieces.
6. Get a large mixing bowl: Toss in it the pasta, chicken, eggs, cucumber, radishes, carrots, green onions, and red onion. Add the Italian dressing and mix them again.
7. Place the salad in the fridge for 1 h 15 min.
8. Place lettuce hearts in serving plates. Divide the salad between them. Serve them right away.
9. Enjoy.

Romano Linguine
Pasta Salad

Prep Time: 15 mins
Total Time: 35 mins

Servings per Recipe: 6
Calories	275 kcal
Fat	12.8 g
Carbohydrates	32.2g
Protein	9.9 g
Cholesterol	10 mg
Sodium	141 mg

Ingredients

1 (8 oz) package linguine pasta
1 (12 oz) bag broccoli florets, cut into bite-size pieces
1/4 C. olive oil
4 tsp minced garlic
1/2 tsp red pepper flakes
1/2 C. finely shredded Romano cheese

2 tbsp finely chopped fresh flat-leaf parsley
1/4 tsp ground black pepper
salt to taste

Directions

1. Cook the pasta according to the directions on the package.
2. Bring a pot of water to a boil. Place a steamer on top. Steam in it the broccoli with the lid on for 6 min
3. Place a saucepan over medium heat. Heat the oil in it. Sauté in it the garlic with pepper flakes for 2 min.
4. Get a large mixing bowl: Transfer to it the sautéed garlic mix with pasta, broccoli, Romano cheese, parsley, black pepper, and salt. Mix them well.
5. Adjust the seasoning of the salad. Serve it right away.
6. Enjoy.

SAUCY CHEDDAR
Fusilli Salad

Prep Time: 15 mins
Total Time: 1 hr 35 mins

Servings per Recipe: 10
Calories	597 kcal
Fat	34 g
Carbohydrates	43.2g
Protein	29.9 g
Cholesterol	85 mg
Sodium	1541 mg

Ingredients

2 tbsp olive oil
1 tsp salt
1 (16 oz) package fusilli pasta
2 lb extra lean ground beef
1 (1.25 oz) package taco seasoning mix
1 (24 oz) jar mild salsa
1 (8 oz) bottle ranch dressing
1 1/2 red bell peppers, chopped
6 green onions, chopped

3/4 C. chopped pickled jalapeno peppers
1 (2.25 oz) can sliced black olives (optional)
1 (8 oz) package shredded Cheddar cheese

Directions

1. Place a large pot over medium heat. Fill it with water and stir into it the olive oil with salt. Cook it until it starts boiling.
2. Add the pasta and boil it for 10 min. Remove it from the water and place it aside to drain.
3. Place a large pan over medium heat. Brown in it the beef for 12 min. Discard the excess grease.
4. Add the taco seasoning and mix them well. Place the mix aside to lose heat completely.
5. Get a large mixing bowl: Mix in it the salsa, ranch dressing, bell peppers, green onions, jalapenos, and black olives.
6. Add the pasta with cooked beef, Cheddar cheese, and dressing mix. Stir them well.
7. Place a piece of plastic wrap over the salad bowl. Place it in the fridge for 1 h 15 min. Serve it.
8. Enjoy.

Creamy Penn
Pasta Salad

Prep Time: 20 mins
Total Time: 2 hrs 27 mins

Servings per Recipe: 10
Calories	381 kcal
Fat	15.5 g
Carbohydrates	34.1g
Protein	25.5 g
Cholesterol	102 mg
Sodium	210 mg

Ingredients

1 (16 oz) box mini penne pasta
1 1/2 lb chopped cooked chicken
1/2 C. diced green bell pepper
2 hard-boiled eggs, chopped
1/3 C. grated Parmesan cheese

1/3 C. chopped red onion
1/2 (8 oz) bottle creamy Caesar salad dressing, or to taste

Directions

1. Cook the pasta according to the directions on the package.
2. Get a large mixing bowl: Toss in it the pasta, chicken, green bell pepper, eggs, Parmesan cheese, and red onion.
3. Add the dressing and stir them well. Cover the bowl and place it in the fridge for 2 h 15 min. Adjust the seasoning of the salad and serve it.
4. Enjoy.

HERBED FETA
and Roasted Turkey Salad

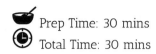 Prep Time: 30 mins

Total Time: 30 mins

Servings per Recipe: 8	
Calories	767 kcal
Fat	65.3 g
Carbohydrates	24.6g
Protein	21.4 g
Cholesterol	59 mg
Sodium	1270 mg

Ingredients

1 1/2 C. olive oil
1/2 C. red wine vinegar
1 tbsp minced fresh garlic
2 tsp dried oregano leaves
3 C. Butterball(R) Golden Oven Roasted
Turkey Breast, sliced thick and cubed
3 C. cooked penne pasta
1 (16 oz) jar pitted kalamata olives,
drained, chopped

1 pint grape tomatoes, halved
8 oz crumbled feta cheese
1 (5 oz) package spring lettuce mix
1/2 C. chopped Italian parsley
1/2 C. thinly sliced red onions

Directions

1. Get a small mixing bowl: Combine in it the olive oil, vinegar, garlic and oregano. Mix them well to make the vinaigrette.
2. Get a large mixing bowl: Toss in it the rest of ingredients. Add the dressing and mix them again. Adjust the seasoning of the salad then serve it.
3. Enjoy.

Nutty Tuna and Pasta Salad

Prep Time: 25 mins
Total Time: 45 mins

Servings per Recipe: 6
Calories   906 kcal
Fat   49.3 g
Carbohydrates   66.9g
Protein   50.8 g
Cholesterol   85 mg
Sodium   672 mg

Ingredients

1 head broccoli, separated into florets
1 lb penne pasta
1 lb fresh tuna steaks
1/4 C. water
2 tbsp fresh lemon juice
1/4 C. white wine
4 medium tomatoes, quartered
1 lb mozzarella cheese, diced
8 large black olives, sliced

1/2 C. walnut pieces, toasted
4 cloves garlic, minced
2 tbsp chopped fresh parsley
4 anchovy fillets, rinsed
3/4 C. olive oil

Directions

1. Cook the pasta according to the directions on the package.
2. Bring a salted pot of water to a boil. Cook in it the broccoli for 5 min. Remove it from the water and place it aside.
3. Place a large pan over medium heat. Stir in it the tuna in a with water, white wine, and lemon juice. put on the lid and cook them until the salmon is done for about 8 to 12 min.
4. Bread the salmon fillets into chunks.
5. Get a large mixing bowl: Toss in it the cooked salmon fish with broccoli, penne, fish, tomatoes, cheese, olives, walnuts, garlic, and parsley. Mix them well.
6. Place a large skillet over medium heat. Heat the oil in it. Slice the anchovies into small pieces. Cook them in the heated skillet until they melt in the oil.
7. Stir the mix into the pasta salad and mix them well. Serve your pasta salad right away.
8. Enjoy.

ROASTED
Kalamata Rotini Salad

Prep Time: 40 mins
Total Time: 1 hr 50 mins

Servings per Recipe: 10

Calories	478 kcal
Fat	34.7 g
Carbohydrates	39.9g
Protein	8.4 g
Cholesterol	0 mg
Sodium	1614 mg

Ingredients

1 (12 oz) package tri-colored rotini pasta
1 small head broccoli, broken into small florets
1/2 tsp minced garlic
1 small red onion, diced
1 (12 oz) jar marinated artichoke hearts, drained and chopped
1 (12 oz) jar pitted kalamata olives, sliced
1 (8 oz) jar roasted red bell peppers,

drained, cut into strips
4 Roma tomatoes, diced
1 (12 oz) jar oil-packed sun-dried tomatoes, drained, cut into strips
1 small zucchini, chopped
1 small cucumber, chopped
1 small yellow bell pepper, chopped
2 ripe avocados
1 (16 oz) bottle Greek vinaigrette salad dressing

Directions

1. Cook the pasta according to the directions on the package.
2. Bring a large pot of water to a boil. Place a steamer on it. Cook in it the broccoli for 5 min with the lid on.
3. Clean the broccoli with some cool water and drain it. Chop it and place it aside.
4. Get a large mixing bowl: Combine in it the broccoli with pasta, garlic, red onion, artichoke hearts, kalamata olives, roasted red peppers, Roma tomatoes, sun-dried tomatoes, zucchini, cucumber, and yellow pepper.
5. Mix them well.
6. Get a small mixing bowl: Mash in it the avocado until it becomes smooth. Add the Greek dressing and mix them well until they become creamy to make the dressing.
7. Add the avocado dressing to the salad and toss it well. Adjust the seasoning of the salad and chill it in the fridge until ready to serve.
8. Enjoy.

Nutty Farfalle Salad
with Dijon Dressing

Prep Time: 15 mins
Total Time: 1 hr 30 mins

Servings per Recipe: 8
Calories	505 kcal
Fat	26.7 g
Carbohydrates	50.7g
Protein	18.9 g
Cholesterol	20 mg
Sodium	731 mg

Ingredients

1 1/2 tbsp white sugar
1 tsp salt, or to taste
1 1/2 tsp ground black pepper
1 tsp onion powder
1 1/2 tsp Dijon mustard
2 cloves garlic, chopped
1 1/2 C. chopped fresh basil
1/2 C. chopped fresh oregano
1/4 C. chopped fresh cilantro
2 tsp hot pepper sauce
1/3 C. red wine vinegar

1/2 C. olive oil
1 tsp lemon juice
1 (4 oz) package grated Parmesan cheese
4 roma (plum) tomatoes, chopped
6 green onions, chopped
1 (4 oz) can minced black olives
1 (16 oz) package farfalle (bow tie) pasta
1/2 C. pine nuts
1 C. shredded mozzarella cheese

Directions

1. Get a large mixing bowl: Combine in it the sugar, salt, pepper, onion powder, mustard, garlic, basil, oregano, cilantro, hot pepper sauce, red wine vinegar, olive oil, lemon juice, and Parmesan cheese.

2. Mix them well. Stir in the tomatoes, green onions and olives. Mix them again. Place the mix in the fridge.

3. Cook the pasta according to the directions on the package.

4. Stir the pasta into the salad bowl and mix them well. Top your salad with mozzarella cheese and pine nuts. Chill it in the fridge until ready to serve.

5. Enjoy.

NUTTY GORGONZOLA
Pasta Salad

Prep Time: 20 mins
Total Time: 1 hr 32 mins

Servings per Recipe: 8
Calories	677 kcal
Fat	45.9 g
Carbohydrates	49.8g
Protein	19 g
Cholesterol	45 mg
Sodium	435 mg

Ingredients

1 (16 oz) package penne pasta
2 tbsp canola oil
2 C. fresh spinach - rinsed, dried and
torn into bite size pieces
1 small green bell pepper, cut into 1
inch pieces
1 small red bell pepper, cut into 1 inch
pieces
1 small yellow bell pepper, cut into 1
inch pieces
1/2 C. canola oil

1/4 C. walnut oil
1/3 C. champagne vinegar
2 tbsp honey
2 C. crumbled Gorgonzola cheese
1 C. chopped walnuts

Directions

1. Cook the pasta according to the directions on the package.
2. Place a large pan over medium heat. Cook in it the spinach with a splash of water for 2 to 3 min or until it wilts.
3. Get a large mixing bowl: Toss in it the spinach, green pepper, red pepper, yellow pepper and cooled pasta.
4. Get a small mixing bowl: Combine in it the 1/2 C. canola oil, walnut oil, vinegar and honey. Mix them well.
5. Drizzle the dressing over the pasta salad. Top it with walnuts and gorgonzola cheese then serve it.
6. Enjoy.

Made in the USA
Coppell, TX
09 May 2022

77588283R00033